THE EROS OF REPENTANCE

PRAXIS POCKETBOOKS
NUMBER ONE

THE EROS OF REPENTANCE

ARCHIMANDRITE GEORGE CAPSANIS —
ABBOT OF THE MONASTERY OF OSIOU
GREGORIOU ON MOUNT ATHOS

Four talks on the theological basis of Athonite
monasticism.

Translated by Hieromonk Alexander (Golitzin),
edited by Robin Amis.

PRAXIS INSTITUTE PRESS

Praxis Institute Press,
275 High Road, Newbury,
MA 01951, USA
and
China Hill, Brightling Road,
Robertsbridge, East Sussex,
TN32 5EH, UK

Printed in Great Britain by
BPCC Wheatons Ltd., Exeter

British Library Cataloguing-in-Publication Data:
A catalogue record for this book is
available from the British Library

Library of Congress catalogue card number:
91-60845

ISBN 1-872292-04-6

*To Father George
and the monks of Osiou Gregoriou,
who have so often opened their lives
to a troubled man of the world
... and to the Pacific Coast deanery
of the OCA who first brought this
text to the world*

Four talks on Athonite monasticism

'A God who does not deify man; such a God can have no interest for us, whether He exists or not.'

The first three of these papers were previously published in the USA in Volume One of the Pacific Central Deanery Spirituality series, and in Britain as a series in the magazine 'Orthodox Outlook'. They are copyright to the monastery of Osiou Gregoriou. For this first booklet we are indebted to Archimandrite George Capsanis, Abbot of the monastery of Osiou Gregòriou, on Mount Athos, and to Father Alexander Golitzin, translator of these papers, Father Basil Rhodes, and their fellows of the editorial committee of the Pacific Central Deanery of the Orthodox Church of America, whose efforts have made possible this fine translation, and with whose permission as well as that of Father George himself, it has been published.

CONTENTS

CONTENTS

Mortals, escape with me from a false world!
Christ calls. Away!
Life be our voyage fair,
Safe riding o'er the surge of lies and care!
One quest alone employs the lonely monk;
How he may reach the haven of true peace
Where never comes the strain of breaking hearts.

O happy life, all music, free from sorrow!
Where is the prudent seeker of true gain
Who will part with all the world—
and choose the cross?

Saint Theodore of Studion

INTRODUCTION

'*When the monk possesses the grace of repentance, he knows the true God, and not some idea of God.*'

This book makes the teachings of one of the contemporary abbots of Mount Athos generally available to the English speaking world for the first time. But it is necessary to warn readers that this Athonite Christianity may not be what they are familiar with. In the reviving Athos of the late 20th Century, the theology of the early church — which today is still followed uncompromisingly by the two thousand or so monks of Athos — is just beginning to take forms that can make sense to modern man, and we can understand these ideas only if we study them with care. The danger is that to us in our Western world this view of Christianity may seem as if it — like so much of modern spiritual thought — has been but recently invented. This is not so. The ideas in this book are not the ideas of one man but—in sense and in essence—are the same as those of earlier fathers of the same tradition—some of whom wrote and taught more than fifteen hundred years ago.

The ways of saying these things are sometimes new, but the meanings are never new. Truth does not change. And what questions does this ancient but durable theology answer? The reply you may get to this question will depend to some extent on you: on the degree to which you know yourself and on the amount of effort you are willing to make to understand what is said. But here are a few suggestions: These words can help to explain to us the inner life of the monks and hermits that are still such an ornament to the Eastern Orthodox Church. They can reveal the beliefs, the practices, and the very real and sometimes visible warmth of heart and vitality these practices give rise to in the best of Orthodox monks and nuns. They can even propose answers to many of the more difficult questions of Western theology — some of them questions that are equally important to philosophy. But the primary characteristic of it all is that this is not primarily a theology of words, but of experience ... not a doctrine, but a window onto a method.

A Theology of Experience

At first reading, this view of Christianity may seem perhaps a light and easy view, even sentimental, but if we take a closer view it can be seen that it is a hard and difficult kind of Christianity, so uncompromising a way, that it could not be followed in truth were not the rewards in some way commensurate with the price that must be paid for them.

As a young monk once said, on the mule-track outside the monastery of which Father George, the author of these papers, is Abbot: *'Most of a monk's pleasures are spiritual ones.'*

The theology of Athos — the theology of Father George and of many of his fellow

Abbots on Athos — sometimes seems unfamiliar because it is not a theology of description but a theology of direct spiritual experience, of personal revelation, in which the monk seeks and finally expresses a personal communion with God through Christ, and everything else revolves about this recurrent fact and the efforts needed to sustain it. Indeed, as Father George himself suggests, this book will remain ever incomplete to the reader until he too has some evidence, some personal experience, some small glimpse of that proof which meets the visitor to Athos — as elsewhere in the Orthodox community — in the eyes and attitudes of the monks... for it is certainly true, as is said in the second of the papers in this booklet, that:

'The same peace and joy greatly impress those who visit the Holy Mountain and can discern these qualities in the faces of those monks who are so holy and outwardly deprived of life's pleasures.'

It is this, the character of those who practice it, which underlines so powerfully the fact that the ancient, patristic view of Christianity-as-experience, which is still taught on Athos today, has not lost its validity as an alternative for a modern world fast growing disenchanted with the outcome of its materialism ... and of its materialist religion. That hints that here is something that perhaps can instead provide the source of what we are lacking. As Father George puts it in one of the papers that follows:

'A God who does not deify man; such a God can have no interest for us, whether He exists or not. I believe that this goes far to explain the wave of atheism in the West, as well as the building of science and philosophy on an atheistic foundation.'

Here too we meet a strange paradox: Those who have much invested in definite ideas and opinions are so often strangely hard on those who do not agree with them. Because they have few doubts, those who derive their theology from experience may sometimes be equally uncompromising in statement, yet—

consistent in all other things — they often seem inconsistent by being strangely tolerant and open in their direct relations to others. They distinguish, yet they do not condemn. Father George of Gregoriou is very much of the latter type.

Finally, we should make it plain that these are verbatim reports of addresses by the Abbot. The forms may appear strange. Not surprising, as we will slowly come to realize: these are in effect reports from a different world, a remnant of the different — and less intellectually straitened — Byzantine civilization, which survives with difficulty on the fringes of our own. Secondly, these are verbatim reports of addresses given by Father George to groups within the Orthodox church. Because the purpose of these addresses is similar, there is some repetition within them which, by not being identical, adds to the overall clarity, so that we have not removed it. Any extra explanation can be useful in so difficult a subject.

*From the introduction to the original
Saratoga edition:*

For over a thousand years the twenty
monasteries and many smaller communities
of the Athonite peninsula have served as a
vital — perhaps the vital — centre of Eastern
Orthodox spiritual life and practice. Fifty
generations of Orthodox Christians have
regarded the 'Holy Mountain' as a beacon
of Christian hope. Its witness to the Spirit of
God in an often dark and hostile world has
drawn pilgrims in hundreds and thousands
to seek and find spiritual comfort, encour-
agement for their lives in the world, and
assurance of the living power of Jesus
Christ.

No understanding of Orthodox monastic
life — or spiritual life generally — is possible
without some grasp of the Church's vision
of man and the meaning of the latter's
salvation in Christ. Abbot George's first
essay lays the essential groundwork for his
theology of monasticism as a faithful expres-

sion of Gospel living, and thus places in their theological context the following articles on the specific role of Mount Athos as it applies to the world of the 1980's.

It may be helpful to summarize briefly the theological background of the author. For Orthodox Christianity, if the meaning of the 'good news' in Christ had to be squeezed into a single word, that word would be theosis: 'deification'. While this term may have a strange, not to say disquieting ring to American ears, it is scarcely foreign in intent to New Testament writings. In 2 Peter 1:4, for example, Christians are bidden to become: '...*partakers in the divine nature.*' Again, our Lord in John 17 (especially vv.5 and 21-25), prays that His followers may acquire the glory '*which was before the world*' through His gift and their union with Him. Later, during the patristic period, Saint Irenaeus of Lyons (2nd Century AD) and Athanasius of Alexandria (4th Century), to name but two, repeat the theme which has echoed ever since in the lives of Orthodox saints: '*God became man*', Saint Athanasius says, '*that man may be made God.*'

The tradition of the Church understands the work of Christ as implicit in the creation of the human race. Man '*Made according to the image and likeness of God*' (Gen. 1:27) had inscribed in his 'blueprint', as the fulfillment of that original plan, obscured beyond apparent recall by the powers of sin and death (Rom. 5:12) that '*the word became flesh and dwelt among us.*' (John 1:14) The birth, death, and resurrection of Jesus Christ, followed by His gift of the Spirit at Pentecost, restored the image of God in us, and made possible our ascent to His likeness. Christ has opened for us once more the way to life, to sharing in His divine glory.

But what has this to do with monasticism? The monastic life now, as well as in its origins some seventeen centuries ago, is nothing more than the attempt to live an authentic and integral Christian life. The first monks, in reply to the increasingly secularized Christian community of the late third and early fourth centuries, asserted their determination to live out Christ's commandments. While never promoting themselves as outside or above the larger Christian community, they serve to remind us of our Lord who truly is—and is to come.

While in the world we may forget, or seek to put off with distracting irrelevancies, fads, or momentary crises the immediacy and the hope of the Kingdom to come, the monks do not. Their whole manner of life constitutes a challenge — even an affront — to worldly patterns of living ... a vital witness to the evangelical truth that *'here we have no abiding city, but we seek the one to come.'* (Heb. 13:14)

Their thirst for sanctity ... has provided us with a continuous stream of saints and prophets, whose very existence bears testimony to the truth that the Kingdom dwells among us even now.

Hieromonk Alexander Golitzin
Marquette University

I

Man As An Image Of God

The Orthodox theology of Christ as the image of God (II Cor. 4:4) and of man as made: *'according to the image of God'* (Gen. 1:26) is fundamental to a proper understanding of what it means to be a human being. *'Made according to the image of God'*, signifies both the origin and goal of our existence, our alpha and omega.

The dynamism of the image, freedom and eros

It has been correctly observed that to be human is to be theological. Therefore *'in order to live authentically, we must live every moment theocentrically.'*

If we deny God, we deny and destroy ourselves.

On the other hand, when we live for God, we open ourselves to a process of development and completion which is infinite. Human existence owes its dynamism and its greatness to its '*iconic*' character. So far as we 'image forth' the wise and creative God, so far do we discover in ourselves the charisms of knowledge and creativity.

The same holds true for the quality of freedom: to be the image of God who is free, means that we possess freedom: liberty. According to Saint Maximus the Confessor: '*If we are made according to the image of the blessed and supersubstantial divinity, and if the divine nature is by definition free, then we too, as true image of the divine nature, are by nature free.*' Saint Maximus the Confessor (d. AD 662) By the same reasoning, if our freedom is lost then we too are lost.

Saint Nicholas Cabasilas writes: '*It is the same to say that "freedom is destroyed" as to say: "the destruction of man".*'

But what — more than anything else — manifests the imprint of God on the human soul is the power of desire (eros) within the soul ... and the impetus which a sanctified eros lends the soul in its movement towards its divine archetype. The saints, especially Maximus the Confessor and Dionysius the Areopagite, understand this power of eroticism as not referring simply to human sexual desire.

To put it better, the sexual urge is an expression of that natural yearning which is implanted within us by our creator, and leads us toward Him.

To quote Saint Maximus once again: '*At times scripture refers to God as desire (eros), and at other times as love (agape), and at still other times as the desirable, and the beloved. Being Himself desire and love, he moves toward us while, as desirable and beloved, He moves all those creatures toward himself who are capable of desiring and loving. It is thus that the great apostle, Saint Paul, having come into possession of divine desire, and become a participant of the ecstatic power, cries out inspired: "I live", he says, "yet not I, but Christ lives in me." He speaks as a lover and—as he says himself—as one caught up in the ecstasy of God. No longer living his own life, but instead that of the beloved, which alone is beauty surpassing speech.'*

Therefore we understand the erotic power of the soul, at its deepest level, to be our thirst for the depths of our own being. That thirst can only be slaked when we achieve the goal for which we were made: union with our Archetype, with God—what the Orthodox tradition calls 'deification'.

We can find no rest in created things which pass away. Saint Nicholas Cabasilas says: *'...the thirst of human souls requires infinite waters.'* Saint Augustine adds: *'Our hearts can have no rest until they rest in Thee.'*

We were created to be united with the uncreated grace of God, to become ourselves gods by grace. Here, in a single view, is the mystery of how we can understand the human being as one 'commanded to be God.'

Saint Gregory Nanzianzus, called 'the Theologian', writes on the mystery of man: *'The creator Word ... fashions man as a simple living being from both invisible and visible nature ... and places him on earth as a kind of universe in miniature, another angel, a pilgrim blended of the two worlds, the overseer of the visible creation and the initiate of the spiritual, a king, ruling from above all things on earth ... an animal, making its home here, yet translated elsewhere and —the goal of the whole mystery—by his yearning for God, he is made God.'*

Loss of the image, and its recovery in Christ

With the fall of man, the image of God in him is darkened. Human nature, according to Saint Cyril of Alexandria, has been 'infected' by sin. As a result of this illness, that within us which is *'according to the image'* is incapable of fulfilling itself, of becoming the likeness of God. Jesus Christ, as the radiant and unchanged icon of God, and as the archetype of man, re-establishes the

5

fallen image of Adam with his saving economy. He reveals our original beauty. He is also the good teacher Who re-orients, draws, and guides us toward our divine archetype.

The church summarizes the salvation effected in Christ in her liturgy. An example, from the Vespers of the Transfiguration (August 6th): *'Transfigured, Thou hast made the nature darkened in Adam radiant once again, O Christ, transforming it into the glory and brilliance of the Godhead.'*

When we thus become: *'conformed to the image of Christ'* (Rom. 8:29), we come into possession of our own true form, our genuine humanity.

The fellowship of deification

In the sacraments, the union of God and man through the Lord Jesus Christ becomes a true communion of life, of resurrection, of transfiguration, of our transformation into Christ, and our deification. In this way our likeness to the image becomes actual rather than potential. The believing, faithful, and struggling human being is deified. Deification is not some idealistic desire, but a reality.

First to be deified was the most holy Mother of God. According to our theologians she alone is found at the boundary beyond created and uncreated nature. She alone is god directly after God, and has the second place after the Holy Trinity.

The saints possessing divine eros have also been deified. All the saints live the saying of Saint Ignatius the God bearer: '*My eros has been crucified.*' The relation of the saints to God is erotic, i.e., desiring or yearning, not simply ethical. The grace of deification shines in their faces, and is revealed in their bodies which smell sweetly, give forth myrrh, remain uncorrupted, and work miracles. The Orthodox Church is the place and fellowship of deification.

Whatever takes place in Orthodoxy is deifying, i.e., given to bring us into communion with God. The holy icons of Christ, of the Mother of God, of the saints, and all the decoration of our Orthodox Churches declare that, truly, *'God has become man in order to raise Adam up a God.'* Deification is possible because grace is an uncreated and divine activity, able thus to deify us. Deification is effected by God and 'suffered' by man. Deified man is purified from the passions. Attending to the prayers of the heart, he receives an experience of divine grace which refreshes and comforts him. A most exalted experience of deification is the vision of the light of Mount Tabor, the uncreated light. Deified people not only see this supernaturally, but indeed they are themselves beheld within it — as has been witnessed to in the lives of many saints.

Modern secularism: a false alternative

When human dynamism is not oriented in its proper direction, toward our Maker and Father, then it reveals itself negatively. The faculties of the soul are torn apart. The intellect is darkened. Fed by the passions, the mind hardens, becomes bestial and demonic. According to Saint Gregory Palamas: *'A mind removed from God becomes like either a dumb beast or a demon. Once having transgressed the bounds of nature, it lusts for what is alien. Yet it finds no satisfaction for its greed and, giving itself the more fiercely to fleshly desires, it knows no bounds in its search for earthly pleasures.'*

Without God, the soul tumbles into the abyss of non-being — which finally devours it. The human person, dissolving, falls to pieces. Life becomes a hell, freedom a burden, and other people a curse. The state of fallen human existence is tragic. It has 'no exit'. The mistake of secular humanism in all its shades is that it tries to make us forget our divine origin and purpose; our iconic character. In the name of progress, of civilization, of justice, it confuses us as to what is corruptible, temporary, vain and passing. It cuts off our wings. It strives to confine our divinely-instilled dynamism and erotic thirst to worldly activities—which are not so much evil in themselves as insufficient; too limited to fulfil the desires of living beings who are made by God and for God. It also tries to persuade us that humanity is itself God; its own law, self-sufficient and self-fulfilling.

Here we arrive at the very sin of Adam; self-deification, egoism. Here we find the essence of secularist philosophy, ethics, and politics. This same philosophy is the organization of life outside the Church. Secularism is the product of Western atheism, an illness which is now beginning to devour our own Orthodox people.

Traditional Orthodoxy, our answer and responsibility

We must admit, however, that sometimes there is also an error from our side. Under the influence of Western Christianity, the Orthodox way of deification is often replaced by the 'way of ethical improvement.'

The latter, a vision of natural and ethical deification, is man centred. Even when it has a religious flavor, it still does not differ in essence from the ethical beliefs of atheistic humanism. It is neither churchly nor liturgical. It does not reveal to the world human beings who are deified. Instead it produces, (in Greece at least), 'small-town Christians': people limited to the bounds of propriety as they understand it. It is based on human ethical activity, and not on the action of God's uncreated grace. It does not lead men out of their eccentricity, nor provide them with the experience of divine grace, nor help them advance in true prayer and fellowship with God.

This approach made its first appearance in the Orthodox world some six hundred years ago. It was represented by the Western theologian Barlaam the Calabrian, and it was as opposed to the latter individual that Saint Gregory Palamas made himself the defender of the theology of uncreated grace. Barlaam was defeated. However, he has since returned in the form of the strong intellectual currents out of the West which have been 'flooding' into our Eastern European countries over the past two centuries.

Today we must become aware of the significant difference and opposition which exists between these two anthropologies and ways of life: that which is represented by Barlaam, and that which we find in Saint Gregory and the Philokalia. When our young people wake up from the lethargy of hedonism and humanistic self-deception, they begin to wander in search of a place to rest. A merely conventional Christianity cannot offer them such a place. Their souls thirst for a personal encounter and an experience of God, for a life which embodies a genuine mysticism, a redeemed and sanctified eroticism. If they cannot find true Orthodoxy, cannot come to know our mystical theology, our real tradition and our genuine piety, then they will seek their resting places elsewhere—in the mysticisms of the Far East, for example, or in the much advertised self-transcendence provided by the artificial — and lethal — paradise of drugs ... or in the fogs and bogs of the occult.

It is our responsibility to see that they do not do this.

II

THE THEOLOGICAL WITNESS OF MOUNT ATHOS

The holy mountain of Athos in its entirety, both in its past and in its present, bears witness to Christ. Its witness is one of faith, hope, and love, a witness to life everlasting. This witness of true and evangelical life is thus also a theological witness: '*The accomplishment of purity is the foundation of theology*', says Saint John of Sinai. Permit me to draw attention to some aspects of this witness.

The witness of true repentance

Our Lord, the Word made flesh, began His preaching with an invitation to repentance: '*And after John had been imprisoned, Jesus came to Galilee preaching the word of God and saying:*

"The time is fulfilled and the Kingdom of God is at hand. Repent and believe the Gospel".' (Mark 1:14–15) On Mount Athos, repentance is experienced as the basis of the Christian life. Someone once asked an elder of the Mountain: *'What is the Holy Mountain?'* He replied, *'There is joy in heaven over one sinner who repents, and here we have many who repent.'*

Athos is indeed a place of repentance. Its monks have come here in order to live true repentance, to receive in themselves the depths of their own sinfulness, to suffer on account of it, to find assurance of the Lord's forgiveness, to be cleansed of their passions.

Repentance is the daily struggle of the monk. His asceticism looks toward this one purpose: that he repent the more deeply and so is more pleasing to God. Repentance is the monk's 'science'. He does not repent just because he sinned at some time in the past. Rather, he feels intensely and every day that he cannot reply perfectly to God's love. He wants to offer himself completely to God, to be in perfect harmony with His commandments, and not to embitter Him with the slightest opposition to His will. Neither does the monk desire for even an instant to relax from the remembrance of God. As Saint Gregory the Theologian writes: '*Rather he remember God even than breath.*' Repentance is thus a dynamic condition, a continuous progress towards the Lord. Properly speaking, it is the pursuit of the living God.

Its character is neither primarily ethical nor legalistic. Instead, it is the fruit of a sanctified eroticism which strains toward the beloved Lord, a sign of profound humility and desire for God.

The younger monks on Athos learn from the older fathers who, even when they have attained a high degree of virtue, still repent and still mourn, so that they fulfil the word of the Lord: '*Blessed are those who mourn, for they shall be comforted. Blessed are those who weep now, for they shall laugh.*'

The holy elders instruct the younger men not by calling them to imitate their virtues, but by showing them how much they feel themselves to be sinners and unworthy. Athonites do not pretend to be good.

They are not hypocrites. They reveal what they are. They confess in all simplicity whatever temptation they consider sinful. If, as human beings of flesh and blood, they become the cause of any grief to a brother, they do not rest until they have bowed before him and sought his forgiveness before the day's end.

Our whole climate on Mount Athos calls us to repentance, to spiritual struggle, and to violence within ourselves for the sake of God's Kingdom. How could we rest when we meet daily, when we keep company with brethren who are holy, are prototypes of repentance; when daily at the office so many examples of Christian perfections are set before us. These demand that we struggle not for half-measures but for the perfection which the Lord commands.

One sign of true repentance is blessed compunction, the broken and contrite heart, the constantly flowing tears of those who have progressed in repentance. Very often such fruit cannot be hidden. This kind of repentance draws down the grace of God, secures the penitent, and brings peace and spiritual joy to his soul. The same peace and joy greatly impress those who visit the Holy Mountain, and are able to discern these qualities in the faces of those monks ... who are so holy, and outwardly deprived of life's pleasures.

A characteristic of the monk who lives in repentance is his attribution of every good thing to God. Depending on divine grace for everything, he has been stripped of every human self-sufficiency, every confidence in self, and every desire to please himself. Those who possess the spirit of repentance and humility will normally withdraw from giving advice.

Even should they do so, it will be out of love and obedience, and not because they feel themselves to be worthy of it. Should you ever visit or live for a time on Mount Athos, you will find yourself in a place of repentance, where human incapacities, imperfections, and sins may not be lacking, but where everyone is yet in complete harmony on the goal of life; to cleanse oneself of discord, of willfulness and self-love in order to fulfil the commandments of the Saviour. You will yourself feel the need to repent, to confess, to struggle.

It has often been observed that many of those who come to the Holy Mountain with no intention of confessing, will confess while they are there, and that while on the Mountain others who confess regularly while in the world, find themselves confessing sins of which they had either been unconscious or had not had the courage to confess before. There is indeed much joy in heaven when every day on Athos many sinners repent, both monks and pilgrims who, making their peace with God, become His friends. In this fashion the Holy Mountain makes its silent proclamation of repentance, and reminds us all that true repentance does not exhaust itself in some ethical and pharisaic self-justification. Neither can it be divided up into single moments. Instead, it comprises the foundation of the whole of Christian life.

In today's world, psychology, pedagogy, and psychiatry—all of them based on a non-Orthodox Christian anthropology — ignore and are silent about the reality of sin. Yet sin after the fall is an anthropological reality. It does not disappear because we try to persuade ourselves that it does not exist. There exists only one way for man, the creature of God, to find freedom from the guilt and weight of sin: through forgiveness by his Maker and Creator. Then, truly, man is at peace, liberated from the interior contradictions that create in him anxieties, neuroses and psychopathy. Then, indeed, he lives in the freedom of God.

The witness to a living God

'*When the monk possesses the grace of repentance, he knows the true God, and not some idea of God.*'

The God of the Gospels is Immanuel; '*God with us*'. He is with us and we are capable of experiencing Him. Ours is not the unapproachable God of the philosophers. He is not the 'absolute being' of Western scholasticism. Rather, He is God who, while abiding unapproachable in His secret essence, yet comes forth out of Himself by His active will and infinite love, to meet and unite Himself with man. The distinction between God's hidden being and His active presence has always been maintained by the Orthodox Church. However, while it appears in the works of many Fathers, it was the Athonite saint, Gregory Palamas, who first taught it systematically in the 14th Century, in order to defend the reality of the saints' experience of God as light. Saint Gregory's teaching was quickly and formally accepted by the Church, who recognized in his writings its own faith. We feel it no exaggeration to say that this saint's teaching is a great blessing for the world. Why? Because it insists that the believer, once having become cleansed of the passions and having become a participant in the holy sacraments, is capable of receiving a direct experience of God, of seeing the uncreated light of the Holy Trinity — the same light which the Apostles beheld at the Lord's Transfiguration on Mount Tabor.

(Matt. 17:1–8; Mark 9:2–8; Luke 9:28–36)

God enters the world through his uncreated energies. He thus endows it with existence, preserves and directs it. He is present in His creation.

If, however, God were essence, or being alone, without His divine energies, if grace were a created thing—as Western Scholastics tell us — then man would be incapable of knowing Him directly, of seeing Him, of becoming a God himself, for a created thing (grace) cannot deify the creature (man). Neither could God Himself be present within creation, nor could He be personally at work within it. Just as the relentless laws of nature must replace an uncreated joy not present in nature, even so the absence of uncreated grace from the life of the Church and of Christians creates a need for an ethical and legal system whose head is the Pope.

A God who does not deify man; such a God can have no interest for us, whether He exists or not. I believe that this goes far to explain the wave of atheism in the West, as well as the building of science and philosophy on an atheistic foundation. It is surely a sorry thing that we Orthodox also, influenced by Western Europe, are ignorant of and indeed sometimes even condemn Saint Gregory Palamas and other Fathers of the Church. This results in our substituting ethical conduct and a rationalistically idealist theology for the ascetical and pastoral Orthodox teaching of deification. The former approach leads directly to an 'accidental Christianity' and finally to atheism.

Many of our young people, weary of both materialism and ideology, are seeking mystical experience either in the teachings of oriental religions or in the artificial paradise of drugs. Why this drift? Because they think that Orthodoxy is exclusively a matter of ceremonial and public declarations. They are ignorant of the mystical and sober tradition of the Philokalia, of the prayer of the heart which affords believers entry into the experience of the divine: '*Blessed are the pure in heart, for they shall see God.*'

Yet this way of prayer is still taught on Athos today. We know it as the way of revelation within the heart, within the centre of each person's being. It is a cleansing of the passions, a turning of the mind inward into the heart, the union of heart and mind with Christ by which the union with God may afterward follow the witness of a way of life centered on the God-man, Christ.

Repentance and knowledge of the living God permit the Christian, and particularly the monk of Athos, to direct his freedom toward the actual centre and source of life, the triune God. If one would live not anthropocentrically but theocentrically, he must centre his life on Christ.

When someone lives centered on God he lives 'eucharistically'. That is to say; he receives other people and the things of life as God's gifts to his life. He gives both to the Lord with thanksgiving, in return offering his own self to God, and to God's children. In the bread and wine of the Eucharist, which are the gifts of God, the Christian offers his whole self and world back to God. The bread and wine summarize what we are, and what we live by: '*Thine own of thine own we offer to Thee, through all and for all.*'

The Lord receives our gifts and offers us in return His own Body and Blood, i.e. His Life. Thus the life of God becomes our life. As communicants of the divine life, we are enabled to live authentically ... truly spiritually.

God in Christ, who is sacrificed and offered for us, gladdens the Christian as he partakes of the Eucharist, and so he helps him to attain the divine 'likeness' — which is the sharing in Christ's sacrifice of love offered to His brethren. Therefore, to say that: '*I live theocentrically*', means that I live eucharistically, liturgically, ecclesiastically, sacrificially.

The mind of our present age is anthropocentric. It is thus neither eucharistic, nor liturgical, nor sacrificial. It is not characterized by love of God or of brother, but only by a tenderness for one's own self. Our whole civilization is built upon self-love.

It is natural, if Christians are influenced by this prevailing anthropocentricity, that they will live in a divided manner as a result. Sometimes they might behave 'religiously', (while they are attending Church services), but at other times (outside the Church building), they act as if they were indifferent to the Faith. Religiosity itself, the manner of Christian piety, departs from the traditional churchly and Orthodox way. It becomes instead individualistic. Sentimentality replaces sobriety. The liturgical life and worship of the Church are seen as something good but as of secondary importance. We come no longer to perceive that — outside the Liturgy and the Church's worship — the world is incapable of being unified and transfigured in newness of life. We attempt to replace the activity of God in the Church and her liturgical life with our own activity on behalf of the world, whether through social action or via political struggle. We try to make the Church an instrument for helping and improving the world, when in fact it is for the world to become Church, to be grafted into the Body of Christ, to die and so to be raised up.

We may be sure that behind this state of affairs lies our wish to be accepted by our secularized society. The latter does accept, even applauds people of the Church, when they work according to the world's agenda— instead of the Church's.

Western humanism has altered the perception of many Orthodox people. So much is this so that we are no longer sensitive to the spiritual tradition of our God-bearing Fathers, of monasticism, iconography, traditional chant, the lives of the saints, architecture, the conciliar liturgy of the Church's body, the holy canons, the teachings, and the true piety of Orthodoxy. In this way, though, neither we nor the surrounding world are 'made Church'. Neither of us is saved: '*What is not assumed is not healed.*' We remain scattered, and neither we nor the surrounding world live united in Christ. We do not know Him within ourselves.

By God's grace however, the Christocentric tradition of the Church as life and way of life is preserved among the monks. The heart of the Tradition is the Holy Trinity in Christ. The purpose of the

Tradition is union with God. All of life is referred to and re-created in God.

The Divine Liturgy is celebrated daily. Worship occupies the first place. Work, duties, eating, hospitality — all begin from and return to the Holy Eucharist. Everything becomes Eucharist. The location of the monastery Church in the physical centre of the compound, and the ordering of all the buildings around the altar, reveal this fact. The monk remains in continuous union with the Lord through his unceasing practice of the Jesus prayer: '*Lord Jesus Christ, have mercy on me a sinner.*' Thus he unites the faculties of his soul, so that even at work he struggles to pray that: '*Christ might be all in all.*' As Saint Symeon of Thessalonica writes: '*For he is a Christian who is wholly with Christ, thinking about Christ ... and in relation to Christ studying, caring, living, and being moved to act. He breathes only Christ, and carries Him about with himself, neither having nor desiring anything save Christ. As did the Apostle Paul, he holds Christ alone as his reward. Christ is to him the pearl of great price, his great treasure and life and light, his sweetness and kingdom everlasting.*' (Saint Symeon of Thessalonica)

Should one find oneself on the Holy Mountain of Athos, he would discover a new way of perceiving; a whole different world with different standards, different goals belonging to another kingdom — indeed, to the Kingdom which is to come. We say that he shares in and tastes the Kingdom.

At this point he becomes aware that the anthropocentric standards and goals of the world cannot be salvific — cannot save. He senses the necessity of conforming his own life to the standards of Athos, standards which are none other than the Christocentric standards of Orthodoxy. It is in this fashion that the lives of many pilgrims to Athos have been changed. After their pilgrimages they begin to practice a Christianity which is more Churchly, more traditional — more Orthodox — than before.

The same people also uncover the meaning of many of the Church's rules and traditions, which previously they had ignored or been ignorant of: of liturgical life, of fasting, vigil, prayer of the heart, and of stillness as the precondition of prayer. Certainly, Christians in the world cannot live precisely as monks. They can however live in accordance with the spirit and standards of monastic life. This will aid them greatly in preserving their own inner unity and balance while living in a troubled and anxious world.

The witness to an Orthodox society

The Holy Mountain bears witness to the hidden life in Christ. At the same time, its testimony is to the evangelical manner of organizing life in society. This is no paradox. In a very essential way, interior life is also social life, since through it a man truly communicates with God and with his fellows. As we read in the Acts of the Apostles: *'And all that believed were together and had all things in common, and sold their possessions and goods and parted them to all men, as every man had need. And they, continuing daily with one accord in the temple, and breaking bread from house to house, did eat their food with gladness and singleness of heart, praising God and having favour with the people.'* (Acts 2:44–47).

This blessed common society of the Jerusalem Christians still continues, by grace of God, in the common-life monasteries which form the foundation of monasticism on Mount Athos. Here the monastic tables are set daily with love not only for the monks, but also for the flood of pilgrims and visitors who come to the holy places. This occurs only on Mount Athos, and it occurs because of the sacrifice and labour of the brothers. Here we divide our spiritual and material goods with our brethren in the name of Christ. You will find that on Athos the Church is not a closed circle where others have no place, but rather as it appears on the icon for the feat of Pentecost, an open hemisphere, a welcoming embrace, which invites and has room for all the world.

Saint Basil the Great, legislator and theologian of the common life, writes concerning the Christian society: '...*I call that a most perfect community of life in which private property has been expelled, conflict of will chased away, where every kind of turbulence, aggression, and quarrel has been trampled under foot; but where instead all is in common; souls, wills, bodies, and everything which is required for the nurture and care of bodies, where God is in common. Common the goods of piety, salvation in common, common the struggles, the labours, and the crowns, where the many are one and the one is not alone but among many. Where is the equal of this way of life? What is there greater? ... All are equally servants and lords of one another ... love itself subordinating them one to another ...*' (Saint Basil the Great) Thus do the monks return again through love to the condition of Adam before the Fall, when sin had not yet broken up the unified nature of man. They imitate precisely the life of Christ with the choir of the Apostles, '*where all is common*', and where to the Apostles in common Christ provided himself. They are zealous for the life of the angels, '*preserving all in common just as the latter.*'

The unity of the monks reveals to men how many good things the incarnation of the Saviour has brought to us: '*For this is the sum of the saviour's economy according to the flesh, that he might join human nature to itself and to Himself, removing the cleft wrought be evil and recalling the original union, just as some wonderful physician might take a body cut in pieces, and with saving medicines bind it again together, and make it alive.*' (Saint Basil the Great)

Saint Basil's theological and Christological perspective on the common life is characteristic of the tradition. The saint always speaks of the common life as anchored in the rock which is Christ.

It is relative to this love, unity, and possession in common that Christian societies in the world must orient themselves if they wish to fulfil the Gospel of Christ. In the common life of monasticism, one may find the principles for the saving solution of our social problems, a true and human solution which will not overlook the spiritual and God-like nature of man.

The monk who is voluntarily humble, without private possessions, and subordinate to obedience — all after the example of the Saviour—proclaims to the world silently yet with great force the realities of faith, sacrifice, humility, love, justice, and peace as the prerequisites for true freedom.

The witness to the Orthodox Faith

The witness of the Holy Mountain is also precious because it concerns the themes of the Orthodox Faith. The struggle of the Holy Fathers of our Church was to preserve the Faith once delivered to them without innovation. They knew that any 'forgery' in this realm, be it ever so small, leads to greater forgeries, and that dogma, once it errs, leads to a mistaken life and pastorate. This is gambling with man's salvation.

Today, under the influence of secularization, the dogma and traditional Orthodox exobiology of the Church are overlooked. The unity of the 'churches' is being pursued along practical and pragmatic lines, without thought for the necessary unity in Faith. One old Athonite elder has said, wisely and simply, that: *'The dogmas are not for the Common Market.'* Another has said: 'How can we accept the Latins without their changing in any regard while at the same time we light the lamp every day at the icon on the spot where the martyr-monks were put to death who reproved the Latins? These martyrs we honour as saints.'

The Fathers of the Holy Mountain often say as well; *'If we should be silent about the Faith which is in danger, how can we explain to ourselves our sitting so many years on this rock?'*

It is a fact that whoever struggles for precision in the life in Christ is also sensitive to the teachings of piety. The monks have the experience of Christ who is Truth in person. They cannot be dissuaded from this Truth in its dogmatic formulation.

The Church has always taken account of this sensitivity of the monks. Wise and holy monks — men such as Saint Maximus the Confessor — have stood as pillars and exemplars of the Orthodox Faith, and directed the work of Œcumenical Councils. See what the great saint and lamp of the Church, Theodore the Studite, says: '*If, then, monks are something in the present times, let them be proven by their works. The work of the monk is not to cleave to some newly risen innovation of the Gospel, because in setting an example of heresy for the laity and keeping company with heretics they will be obliged to give account for the destruction of the faithful.*' (Theodore the Studite)

Elsewhere the same saint writes: '... *And overlooking others, let me come to the present generation and the heresy which confronts us now. Who have resisted unto blood, struggling against sin, if not the blessed Fathers of this and of other monasteries? Such then are the accomplishments and victories of the monks, and monks are the nerves and foundation of the Church. Such indeed and so great is the dignity with which we have been graced by the goodness of God.'* (Theodore the Studite)

The struggle of the Athonites is certainly not directed primarily against heresy. It is a struggle to realize in themselves — and to make manifest—the fullness of the Truth and the Life possessed by the Church. The labour, the disquiet, the protests of the Holy Mountain are finally elements of the struggle for fullness, for catholicity. It is in order that the preaching of the Cross not be emptied, that the Gospel not be counterfeited. In the words of Saint Gregory the Theologian, we must not theologize in the manner of Aristotle, (scholastically), but according to the fishermen (apostolically.) Athos bears its witness in order that we not lose the possibility of deification and of the Uncreated Light by accepting grace as a created thing; that the Church not fall from being the 'Body of Christ' to become some human organization; that some 'infallible' Pope not come to replace the truly infallible, illuminating, and uncreated grace of the

Holy Spirit, Who is ever present in the Church.

For these reasons, by the grace of God, we, together with the holy bishops, clergy, and faithful people in the world, shall never agree that there should come about the least alteration in the dogmas of piety. We take this attitude out of love: love for the God of Truth and for the non-Orthodox who are not helped when they are prevented from coming into confrontation with the Truth which saves: '*You will know the Truth, and the Truth shall make you free.*'

Summary: Athos, the Cry of the bride

One cannot know the Holy Mountain with one or two visits. Much more is it impossible for someone to know it, if he approaches it with the proud logic of the world: '*Blessed are the poor in spirit, for theirs is the Kingdom of heaven.*'

As far as the Athonite monk is poor, so much the more deeply is he initiated into the mystery of the Holy Mountain. When Jacob saw the ladder which led to God and the angels who ascended and descended from heaven, he said: *'How fearful is this place! Is this not the house of God and this the gate of heaven?'* Jacob wrestled with God. On Athos the monks wrestle with God. They speak with God, with the Mother of God, with the saints. Thus they truly witness to God and to His love in Christ for the world.

All of us perceive that Mount Athos is more meaningful than some huge outdoor museum of Byzantine art and civilization. It is the dew of Hermon descending on Zion. It is the comfort of our hearts, a lamp at our feet. We feel as well that Athos does not live for itself, but for the Church. It is God's gift to the Church—and the Church's gift to God. It is not above the Church, but a manifestation of her life. Praise of the Holy Mountain is praise of our Mother, the Church.

Athos keeps vigil, serves, is silent, and prays. Through the prayerful silence of the Holy Mountain one may hear the cry of the Bride to her Bridegroom: *'And the Spirit and*

the Bride say, Come. And let him that heareth say, Come. And let him that is athirst, come. And whosoever will, let him take the water of life freely ... He which testifieth these things saith, surely I come quickly. Amen. Even so, come, Lord Jesus.'
(Rev. 20:17–20)

III

EVANGELICAL MONASTICISM

A new life in Jesus Christ

The Gospel of our Lord Jesus Christ is a 'god-spell' or 'good news' because it brings to the world something which is not merely new teaching, but a new life in contrast to the old. The old life is ruled by sin, passions, corruption and death, and is presided over by the devil. In spite of all its 'natural' pleasures it still leaves a bitter taste, because it is not true life, the life for which man was made, but a corrupted life, diseased, characterized by a sense of the irrational, of emptiness, and of anxiety.

The new life is offered to the world by the God-man Christ as a gift and possibility for all men. The believer is united with Jesus

Christ, and thus partakes of His divine and immortal life, that is, of everlasting or true life.

A life of repentance

In order for the believer to be joined to Christ and to be made alive, he must first die to the old man by means of repentance. One must crucify and bury the old man, (that is, egoism, the passions, and the selfish will,) at the cross and tomb of Christ, in order to rise with Him and walk in 'newness of life' (Rom. 6:4). This is the work of repentance and the carrying of the cross of Christ. Without repentance, the continual crucifying of the old man, the believer is incapable of believing evangelically. He cannot give himself entirely to God and: *'love the Lord with all his heart, and all his soul, and all his mind, and all his strength.'* (Mark 12:30)

It is for this reason that the Lord Himself set forth as the foundation of His preaching, and as the basis of faith, repentance: *'repent, and believe in the Gospel.'* (Mark 1:15) He did not hide the fact that the life of repentance is a difficult and uphill struggle: '*Narrow is the gate and hard is the way which leads to life*.' (Matt. 7:14)

To walk this way means to lift up the cross of repentance. The old man does not give way without violence, and the devil is not conquered without hard warfare.

The monk promises—throughout his life—to follow the narrow and hard way of repentance. He breaks away from the things of the world, in order to achieve the one thing which he desires. He dies in relation to the old life, that he may live the new one which Christ offers him in the Church. The monk pursues perfect repentance by means of continual asceticism: vigils; fasting; prayer; the cutting away of his will, and unquestioning obedience to his elder. In the practice of these he forces himself to deny his private and selfish will, and to love God's will. A monk is 'a perpetual forcing of nature'. The word of the Lord is thus fulfilled: '*The kingdom of heaven is taken by violence, and the violent take it by force*.' (Matt. 11:12)

In the midst of the birth-pangs of repentance, the new man according to God is slowly begotten. Belonging to the struggle of repentance is the effort of continually guarding one's thoughts. It is by putting away from one's self all the evil and demonic temptations that act to soil the mind, that one is able to keep the heart pure, and it is such a heart that reflects God. In the words of our Lord: *'Blessed are the pure in heart, for they shall see God.'*

Victory over egoism and the passions makes the monk calm, meek, and humble, in a word—*'poor in spirit'*—and a participant in all virtues of the Beatitudes. It also makes him a 'child', like that child which Jesus blessed and whom He called on all to imitate if they wished to enter His kingdom.

The whole life of the monk becomes a study of repentance, his way of life a way of repentance. A monk is a scientist of repentance, one who is: *'branded with the life of repentance'*, (Canon 43, 6th Œcumenical Council) for the whole Church. Contrition and the tears of repentance are the most eloquent sermon.

In addition, the monk's whole manner of life, the way of self-mortification, is a judgement of the world. Again the world, which is silently judged by the monk, does not take part in his repentance. It rejects him, it hates him, it despises him, and it sees him as a fool. Yet, with such men: *'the foolish, the weak, the ignoble and rejected of the world'*, the wisdom of the 'wise' is put to shame by God (1 Cor. 1:27).

For those who do not partake of his spirit, the monk's hidden and secret life is a mystery sealed with seven seals. Those who do not (share in this) see him as no use either for society or for the missionary work of the Church. His life is hidden with Christ in God, though it shall be revealed in glory with the coming of Christ (Col. 3:4).

Only if the heart of a man is continually being purified of egoism, of selfishness, and of the passions, is it capable through repentance of truly loving God and man. Egotism and love are incompatible. The egotist may often think that he loves, but in fact his 'love' is merely a disguised egotism, hiding (often even from himself) his selfishness and self-interest.

The patient monk is aflame with divine desire. Love of God possesses his heart. He can no longer live for himself, but only for God. Like a bride, the monk's soul longs continuously for the Bridegroom. It cannot rest until it is united with Him. The monk finds no peace in loving God as would a servant—from afar—nor as a hired hand—for the sake of the reward of paradise; he wants to love Him as a son, from a pure heart. *'I no longer fear God, because I love Him'*, says Saint Anthony the Great.

The more the monk repents, the more his desire grows for the love of God. The more he loves God, the more deeply he repents.

A life of prayer and worship

Tears of repentance kindle the fire of love. The monk feeds his desire for the Lord with prayer, especially that spiritual and unceasing prayer which is the continual invocation of the sweetest Name of Jesus.

The prayer: '*Lord Jesus Christ, Son of God, have mercy on me a sinner*', both purifies and establishes him in union with Christ. Worshipping in Church the monk also gives himself lovingly to God, and God gives himself back to him. The monk spends many hours every day worshipping his beloved Lord in the Temple. His participation in worship is not an 'obligation', but rather a necessity of his soul which thirsts for God. In Athonite monasteries the divine liturgy is celebrated every day. The monks are not compelled to attend the services, however lengthy. Yet they do, for the know nothing better than to be in communion with the Redeemer, the Mother of the Redeemer, and the friends of the Redeemer. Worship is a joy and a festival, an opening-up of the soul, and a foretaste of Paradise. The monks live, in other words, according to the way of the Apostles: '*And all that believed were together,*

*and had all things common... and they, continuing
daily with one accord in the Temple and breaking
bread from house to house, did eat their food with
gladness and singleness of heart, praising God...'*
(Acts 2:44–47).

And after the dismissal of the service, the
monk lives worshipfully: his whole life in the
monastery, the service which he performs,
the refectory, prayer, silence and rest, his
relations with the brethren, and the recep-
tion of guests, are offered as liturgy to the
Holy Trinity.

The architecture itself of the monasteries
bears witness to this reality. From the
Church and its holy altar, all things
proceed, and to them all things return.
The corridors, the cells, everything is
centered on the Catholicon (the church or
temple of the monastery) as a hub.

All of life is offered to God, and becomes
worship. The material elements used in the
worship witness to the Transfiguration of all
life, and of the whole creation by God's
grace. The bread and wine of the Divine
Eucharist, the sanctified oil, the incense, the

sounding-boards (*'semantrons'*) and bells which announce the appointed hours, the candles and the oil lamps which are lit and extinguished at certain times of the service, the movement of the canonarch and the ecclesiarch, and as many other movements and activities as are provided by the age-old monastic *'typika'* (rules), are not mere symbols, nor are they psychological props intended to generate sentimental feelings. Instead, they are signs, echoes, and actual manifestations of the New Creation. Everyone, as many as visit the Holy Mountain, discovers that its worship is not static, but possesses a dynamic character. It is a single motion toward God: together with itself, the soul which ascends to God raises up all creation.

In the Athonite vigil, the believer has a unique experience of grace ... the grace which comes into the world from the redemptive work of Christ.

The believer thus tastes of the highest quality of that life which Christ with His

Church offers to the world. The priority which monasticism gives to the worship of God is a reminder, both in the Church and in the world, that if the Divine Liturgy and worship do not once again become the centre of our life, our world will be unable to be united and transfigured. It will be incapable of surpassing its divisions, its imbalance, its emptiness and death ... in spite of all the prideful, humanistic systems and plans intended to improve it.

Again, monasticism reminds us that the Divine Liturgy and worship are not simply one thing in our life; they are its centre, the source of its renewal and its entire satisfaction.

A life based on love

The love of God has—as a direct fruit—the love of God's image, of man — and of all God's creatures. After many years of asceticism, the monk acquires the 'merciful heart' which God loves. According to Abba Isaac the Syrian, a merciful heart is: '... *a burning of* the heart for all creation, whether for men, for the birds of the air, for animals, for the demons, for every creature. From the memory and contemplation of creatures the eyes stream with tears, and from compassion and pity the heart of the merciful man is moved to grief, and is unable to bear, to see, or to hear of any injury, or of anything grievous occurring in creation.

'It is for this reason that at all times such a man prays with tears for the dumb beasts, for the enemies of the truth, and for those who do him injury. He prays that God may protect them and show them mercy.

He prays even for the creeping things, out of his great pity, which moves his heart abundantly.' (Saint Isaac the Syrian — Discourse 81)

In the Gerontikon, (a collection of sayings and works of the desert fathers or 'elders'), we encounter forms of sacrifice and love which call to mind and manifest the love of Christ. It is mentioned that Abba Agathon said: 'I wish to meet a leper and embrace his body.' 'You know perfect love', commented Saint Isaac the Syrian.

The organization of the common life (cœnobitic) monastery is based on love, according to the model of the first Christian communities of Jerusalem. As the Lord with the twelve, and as the first Christians, so monks, too, have all things in common in Christ. The abbot possesses nothing more than the newest novice. No one has money that he may spend as he wishes; only those funds which he takes as a blessing from the abbot for a particular need.

The possession of all things in common, equality, justice, reciprocal reverence, and the sacrifice of one for all, and of all for each, raises the common life to the level of real love and liberty. As many as have lived, be it only for a few days, in true common-life monasteries, know what a joy is the reciprocal love of the brethren, and how much it refreshes the soul. One has the impression that he is living with the angels.

The organizer of common-life monasticism, Basil the Great, speaking characteristically about the love in Christ which rules in the cœnobia, said: '*What can compare with this form of life? What is more blessed? What is truer than its binding together and its unity? What is more full of grace than the blending of personalities and souls? Men have been moved to come from different tribes and countries to be joined together so truly into one that they appear as one soul having many bodies; as the instruments of a single will. The one who is weak in body has many who bear with him; the one who is ill and frail in his soul has many to care for him and set him aright. They are equally servants one of an other, equally lords one over the other, and with unconquerable liberty they strive to show among themselves the greatest servitude. Theirs is a servitude, however, which is not forced out of some necessity of the kind which causes great anxiety for those who rule, but is rather created out of the joy which comes from freedom of the will. Love leads each man to subordinate himself to the other, and establishes freedom in the individual choice of each. It is thus that God willed us to be from the beginning; for this He created us. Such men restore the ancient beauty, because they redeem the sin of the forefather*

Adam… because there would not have been division, separation, and war among men if sin had not divided nature. These men, then, imitate the Saviour and His incarnate life.

'*Just as He did when He formed the band of His disciples, establishing all things in common among the Apostles, so they keep the strictness of this life as obedient to the abbot, imitating the life of the Apostles and of the Lord. They are zealous for the life of the angels because as those (i.e. the angels), they strictly guard the common life. Among the angels there is neither strife, nor envy, nor dispute.*

'*All things belong to each, and all store up for one another those things which are good.*'

A life of service

In monasteries of the common life, the monks are able to live apostolically, genuinely, the mystery of the Church as the sacrament of communion, and as the union of God and men. They are able to live: '*the unity of the faith and the communion of the Holy Spirit*', which is the petition of all Christians. The monk knows from experience that the Church is not a religious institution, nor a law, but brotherhood in Christ, the body of Christ, the gathering together of the formerly scattered children of God (John 11:52), his family in Christ. This experience of the Church gives the monk his capacity to see his brothers as members of his own body, and to honour them as Christ. This is the source of the ready welcome which he extends to pilgrims and visitors, as well as of his continual prayers with tears on behalf of his brethren, both living and dead, both known and unknown.

The monks also fulfil their love for their brethren in the world in other ways, such as by the spiritual refreshment and comfort which they offer to their brothers. Many who are troubled and tired in their souls run to the monasteries, particularly to the Holy Mountain, to find peace for their souls in proximity to elders and confessors who have already found peace with God. On the other hand, those occasions are not rare where experienced Athonite confessors go out into the world, refreshing and confirming many Christians in the faith.

The venerable Seraphim of Sarov, a great Russian saint of the last century, says typically: *'Be yourself at peace with God, and many will come to find peace near you.'*

The venerable Seraphim was speaking from his personal experience, as well as from the experience of the long spiritual tradition of the Church. It is an observed fact that the further those elders who had found peace with God retreated into the desert, the more the multitudes followed them in order to be edified.

In special circumstances, monks are called by the Lord Himself to take up a broader work of preaching and awakening — as occurred with Saint Cosmas the Aitolian. But they are always called by God, and never call themselves. It would have been impossible for Saint Cosmas to save and to enlighten an enslaved people with his preaching if he had not previously been enlightened and illumined by the age old monastic practice of silence, purification and prayer.

The monk does not seek to save the world through pastoral or missionary activity because, being 'poor in spirit', he feels that he does not have the foundations for saving others before he has been saved himself.

He gives himself to God without plans or hopes for the future. He is always at the disposal of the Lord, ready to attend to His call.

The Lord of the Church invites the workers of his vineyard to work in whatever mode He finds salvific and edifying. He called Saint Gregory Palamas to take up the pastoral protection of the Thessalonians, and to give theological expression to the Orthodox piety of the Fathers.

He called Saint Cosmas to go out and preach in apostolic journeys while he illumined Saint Nicodemus the Hagiorite to preach without going out into the world — by means of the theological and spiritual writings which to this very day lead many souls to God. Other monks were called by the Lord to edify the world with their silence and endurance, by their prayers and their tears, as in the case of the Athonite, the blessed Leontius of Dionysiou, who did not go out of his monastery for sixty years. He remained all that time closed within a dark cell, yet the Lord revealed that the same old monk had received the gift of prophecy, and his body gave forth myrrh after his death.

A life of charismatic witness

Properly, what makes the sanctified monk the world's joy and light is his preservation of the image of God.

In the midst of the unnatural condition of sin which we experience, we forget and lose sight of the measure of the true man. That which man was before the fall, and that which is man deified — that is, the image of God — this is what the sanctified monk reveals to us.

For at least as many as are able to discern the deeper and true human nature, without the prejudices of passing ideologies, the monk remains the hope of mankind. If man cannot be deified — or if we have not personally known deified men — it would be difficult to hope in the possibility that man can surpass his fallen condition, can attain to the purpose for which the good God made him; deification by grace. As John of the Ladder says: '*The angels are light for monks, and their way of life is light to all men.*' (Saint John Climacus — Discourse 26)

Already possessing the grace of deification in this life, the monk becomes a sign and witness of the Kingdom of God in the world. According to the holy Fathers the Kingdom of God is the gift and indwelling of the Holy Spirit. By means of the deified monk, the world is given to know 'in ignorance' — to see 'without seeing' the character and glory of the deified man and of the Kingdom of God which is to come, and which is not of this world.

It is thus through monasticism that the eschatological conscience of the Apostolic Church is preserved in the Church of today. By eschatological conscience, we mean both eagerly awaiting the Lord's coming (*marana tha* : Lord, come!) and the awareness of His mystical presence among us even now; that: '*The Kingdom of God is within us.*'

His charismatic remembrances of death, and his fruitful virginity, extend the monk into the age to come. As Saint Gregory the Theologian teaches: '*Christ is born of the Virgin, and enjoins virginity as that which leads us out of the world, cuts off the world, exchanges one world for another, the present world for the world to come ... turning from that which is, to that which is unseen.*' The monk who lives the life of virginity according to Christ, transcends not only that which is unnatural, but nature itself. Attaining to that which is beyond nature, he partakes of the angelic mode of being concerning which the Lord also spoke: '*For in the resurrection they are neither married nor given in marriage, but are as the angels of God in heaven.'* (Matt. 22:30) Just as the angels, so the monks are not virgins in order to accomplish matters of practical importance for the Church (missionary work, etc.), but in order to worship God in their body and spirit. (1 Cor. 6:20).

Virginity sets a boundary to death. In the words of Saint Gregory of Nyssa: *'Just as in the case of the Theotokos, Mary, death which had reigned from Adam until her, stumbled against the fruit of her virginity as at a rock when it came against her, and shattered round about her; so in the case of every soul which passes through fleshly life in virginity, the power of death is somehow shattered and abolished, as having nowhere to insert its sting.'* (Gregory of Nyssa.)

The evangelical and eschatological spirit which monasticism preserves, also serves to protect the Church in the world from secularization and from allying itself with sinful conditions which are antithetical to the evangelical spirit.

Physically above, and silent but spiritually and mystically in the midst of the Church, the monk preaches as from an elevated pulpit the precepts of Almighty God and the necessity for a wholly Christian life. He orients the world toward the Jerusalem which is on high, and toward the glory of the Holy Trinity as the true and catholic goal of creation.

This is the apostolic preaching which monasticism has authentically preached in every epoch, which grounds the apostolic renunciation of all things in the crucified life of apostolic work. Just as the Apostle, even so the monks, *'having abandoned all things'*, follow Jesus and fulfil his word: *'Everyone who leaves houses, or brothers, or sisters, or father, or mother, or wife, or children, or fields for my Name's sake, shall receive an hundredfold and shall inherit life everlasting.'* (Matt. 19:29)

'Owning nothing and possessing all things', the monks share in the sufferings, the deprivations, the hardships, the vigils, and the worldly insecurity of the holy Apostles.

They are made worthy, however, as were the holy Apostles, of becoming: *'eyewitnesses of His Majesty',* (2 Peter 1:16) and of receiving a personal experience of the grace of the Holy Spirit, so that they are enabled to say not only that: *'Jesus Christ came into the world to save sinners, of whom I am first'* (1 Tim. 1:15), but also that: *'What we have heard we have seen with our eyes, what we have beheld and our hands have touched, concerning the word of life ... And the life has been manifested, and we have seen and we bear witness and declare to you the life everlasting, which was with the Father and has appeared to us'* (1 John 1:1–2).

This vision of the glory of God, and the most sweet visitations of Christ, these justify all the monk's apostolic struggles and make of monastic life the *'true and blessed life'* which he would exchange for nothing other — however lowly he may be, and however short the time he, by God's grace, may have been given to know it.

The monk radiates this grace even to his brothers in the world, so that all may see, may repent, may be consoled, may rejoice in the Lord and glorify the merciful God: *'who gives such authority to men.'* (Matt. 9:8).

IV

THEOTOKOS: GUIDE TO TRUE FREEDOM

(Christmas address, 1986, translated on Athos.)

This year in particular, let us direct our attention to one of the most beautiful idiomela of the Vespers for Christmas:

'What shall we offer Thee, O Christ,
Who for our sakes hast appeared on earth as man?
Every creature made by Thee offers Thee thanks.
The angels offer Thee a hymn; the heavens a star;
the Magi, goats; the shepherds, their wonder;
the earth, its cave: the Wilderness, the manger:
and we offer Thee a Virgin Mother,
O Pre-Eternal God, have mercy on us.'

All God's creation feels the need to thank Christ for His Incarnation, and to offer Him the gift of its gratitude. The angels offer their hymns; they awaited the incarnation of Christ because they loved mankind, and were saddened to see men far from God. With the Incarnation and Resurrection of Christ, the good angels will be stabilized in their goodness, that is, holiness and sinlessness and, even more — beatitude and glory will become their permanent condition.

Non-rational creation suffered and groaned with mankind and awaited with yearning (cf. Rom. 8:19) the liberation of man and of all creation from the decay it inherited with man after his fall and separation from the heavenly Father and creator, the source of life.

Rational man suffered even more, awaiting his liberation. For this reason, mankind offers the highest gift to Christ Who becomes man: His Virgin Mother.

In fact, we men had nothing more honourable to offer God. The *Panaghia* ('Pan Aghia':

'All Holy Mother of God') had already offered herself entirely to God, and as a most pure vessel was ready to receive in her womb her Son and her God and so, at her Annunciation, when Archangel Gabriel told her that she would become the Mother of Christ, she could answer with confidence in God: *'Behold the handmaid of the Lord. Be it unto me according to thy word.'*

Moreover, we could not have offered the Virgin Mary to God if she had not offered herself to God. This free offering of the Virgin made the incarnation of God possible, for God would not violate our freedom by becoming incarnate without our own consent. The Virgin was able to stand before God as our representative, and to say 'Yes' to God. Her deed is a deed of unique responsibility, of love, and of freedom. She gave God what He Himself did not have — human nature — in order that God might give man what he did not have — deification (theosis). Thus the Incarnation of Christ is not only God's free act of offering to man, it is also a free offering from man to God through the Virgin.

This mutual freedom is the prerequisite for love. God offers freely without any necessity, and the Virgin accepts the gift freely, without compulsion. The Virgin could not co-operate with God if she had established her own egotistic satisfaction at the content of her freedom — rather than her offering to God and man. Moreover, the Virgin is always rightly blessed by all generations of Christians, and especially during these holy days, as the: *'cause of the deification of all.'* At the same time, she points out the way of true freedom.

Contemporary man is deluded by the devil and believes—as did Adam and Eve earlier— that his freedom is to be found in his autonomy and in his revolt against God. With this egotistic attitude man loses the possibility of true communion, not only with his God and Father, but also with his fellow men, and he lives as an orphan in an intolerable loneliness, which he experiences as an existential emptiness. A young man who uses drugs assures me that he would stop using them if he could stop trying to fill his existential emptiness with them.

The Virgin Panaghia and her Incarnate Son call us to the freedom of love. This freedom proceeds from the Cross. This is not the easy way of the satisfaction of our passions. It is the hard way of sacrifice, of offering, of victory over egotism.

In the name of this freedom, which we have received from the Gospel of Christ, and from the tradition of our Greek Orthodox people, we cannot accept institutions such as those allowing abortion, which evade the freedom of love and which introduce the 'freedom' of egoism as a way of life. Since we Orthodox Christians have chosen the freedom of love as a way of life in the world, as did the Virgin Mary and her Only-Begotten Son, we have before us a great struggle, for we must strive to acquire this freedom. This is the struggle of the Orthodox Christian. This struggle is a Cross, but it is also a joyful struggle because it carries us to the Resurrection.

In this struggle, which you too will undergo, we pray that our Saviour Jesus Christ, Who was born in a cave, will grant you His grace and blessing, through the intercessions of his most blessed Mother and our Mother, the Lady Theotokos.

INNER CHRISTIANITY

By *Saint Theophan the Recluse*
THE HEART OF SALVATION

trans. Esther Williams, intro by George A. Maloney S.J., commentary by
Robin Amis. The life and teachings of Theophan the Recluse, one of the
greatest and most recent of Russia's masters of the psychology of the
inner life. Explains esoteric doctrines never previously published in
English in ways comprehensible to the modern mind.

208 pages, paperback. $17.95 | £8.95   *ISBN 1-872292-02-X*

THE PATH OF PRAYER

– Four Sermons on Prayer. Translated by Esther Williams, introduction
by Robin Amis with a preface by Margaret, Viscountess Long of Wraxall.
A full introduction to the use of liturgical prayer as a method of spiritual
development by the author of more than half the quotations in 'The Art
of Prayer'.

96 pages, paperback, $7.95 | £5.45   *ISBN 1-872292-14-3*
Hand bound, $10.95 | £8.45   *ISBN 1-872292-13-5*

By *P.D. Ouspensky*
THE COSMOLOGY OF MAN'S POSSIBLE EVOLUTION

Companion volume to Ouspensky's well-known 'Psychology of Man's
Possible Evolution', definitive text only made available in 1989.

128 pages, paperback. £7.50   *ISBN 1-872292-01-1*

THE PSYCHOLOGY AND COSMOLOGY OF MAN'S POSSIBLE EVOLUTION

'Together for the first time:' a Definitive Limited Edition of both texts.

224 pages, hard cover. £14.95   *ISBN 1-872292-00-3*

*These two books by P.D. Ouspensky were published in England by
Agora Books at the request of certain of his senior pupils, and are not
for sale in North America for copyright reasons. They are available in
the UK from Praxis Institute Press, which is now continuing the main
work of Agora Books internationally.*

Boris Mouravieff's
GNOSIS

'Despite this unexpected linkage to the core of the Christian mystery, anyone long-studied in Fourth Way ideas will immediately recognize that this book expresses the very essence of the teaching ... There is no denying the authoritative atmosphere which radiates from every page of this book.' Theodore Nottingham, reviewer, 'In the Work'

'... one of those wonderful volumes that manage to rise above specific traditions to a plane of magnificent clarity. It is a challenging contribution to our literature which left me with a great sense of succour and hope.' Timothy O'Neill, reviewer, Gnosis magazine

VOL. I – THE EXOTERIC CYCLE

translated by S.A. Wissa, edited by Robin Amis. The first really new revelation in nearly 50 years of the ideas described by Gurdjieff as Esoteric Christianity, Mouravieff's Gnosis addresses questions of the development of the heart and of the purpose of human life previously only transmitted orally.

296 pages, paperback $24.95 / £14.95   ISBN 1-872292-10-0

VOL. II – THE MESOTERIC CYCLE

translated by S.A. Wissa, Manek d'Oncieu and Robin Amis, edited by Robin Amis. Volume 2 deals with practical questions, provides new information on the transformation of energies and the sublimation of sex energy, and relates human history to divine purpose in new ways.

304 pages, paperback $24.95 / £14.95   ISBN 1-872292-11-9

Ask your bookseller, or order direct from:

PRAXIS INSTITUTE PRESS
*a division of Praxis Research Institute, Inc.
275, High Road, Newbury, MA 01951, USA
Tel: (508) 462 0563 Fax: (508) 462 2340
and China Hill, Brightling Road, Robertsbridge,
E. Sussex, England TN32 5EH. Tel: 0580 881137*